Traces of a Life

BRAD DREW

Traces of a Life
**MARKS & MUSINGS
IN POETRY & IMAGES 1966 – 2015**

BARDDRIEV PRESS

Copyright © Brad Drew 2015

All rights reserved

First Edition
Paperback

ISBN: 978-0-9944992-2-6

Apart from any fair dealing for the purposes of
private study, research or review, as permitted
under the Copyright Act, no part of this book may
be reproduced by any process without permission.
Copyright of all text and illustrations resides under
the Copyright, Designs and Patents Act with Brad Drew.

Layout and Book Design: Brad Drew
Drawings and prints: Brad Drew
Cover Art and Design: Brad Drew

FOREWORD

Brad Drew traces his earlier life abroad, and his later Australian experience, in various poetic forms.

Initially, in the Japanese forms of the tanka and haiku; later, his poems reach out to us through more familiar English forms, such as sonnets and villanelles.

Brad's love of family is also reflected in his many drawings of family and friends, as well as in various scenes.

Many poems here, muse upon the cost, as well as the pleasures, of loving. The pain of loss and the disturbance of absence are clearly expressed. These too, are enhanced by Brad's artwork, accompanying many poems.

Bruce Dawe

11 February 2016

Traces of a Life

INTRODUCTION

I grew up with books as favourite companions, in genres which became increasingly eclectic in their distribution; but I do not recall having any particular interest in poetry per se during my primary or secondary, nor even my tertiary, education years.

I was the first child, and the only boy, in a brood of four siblings; and as such, had the good fortune to receive three years of my mother's undivided attention. Some of my earliest memories, visually strong down to the details of home and furnishings, are of being held on her lap while she read to me. When the distraction of my first sister arrived, I was to a degree, prepared with a small library of my own: admittedly picture-books in the main, with the few words already committed to memory: pop-up and layered, see-through books, such as one treasured copy of Charles Kingsley's 'The Water Babies'. Come primary school, the library continued to grow, with Enid Blyton's 'Famous Five' reigning supreme, along with Richard Crompton's 'William' books, and some boy called 'Jennings', by Anthony Buckeridge; all this, alongside a 'Treasury of Science' and eventually, "The Supernatural Omnibus': a collection of short stories from many of the classic writers (perhaps the first classics I had ever read, though somewhere in earlier times, there had been various copies of Classics Comics), all in one weighty volume – short stories to send a chill, just before bed. So passed my early youth.

Later, during the secondary school years, study of set texts overshadowed much of my reading for pleasure; which in itself, turned into a general interest in matters like psychology and hypnosis, science and geology. Not all was questing curiosity though: at school, there was the first experience and enjoyment of Shakespeare; in private, there came the discovery of the better, classic science fiction of those times, along with the likes of Agatha Christie and Ion Idriess.

University years followed similar lines, though the scope of extracurricular reading matter became increasingly eclectic, in both fictional and factual content; but still, poetry, for its own sake remained an uncharted territory.

I suppose it was only with the lyrics of some of the more soulful, romantic, even depressive, popular singer-songwriters around the turning of the sixties into the seventies, that I found some impetus to express myself in verse; this of course, was prompted by the presence of a certain girl who captured me absolutely at that time. Romantic interests were nothing new but this was more than noteworthy; perhaps it was just the timing, perhaps it was in fact, the girl; whatever it was, she was the catalyst who swept me in her wake, to London and gave birth to an active interest in poetry. I never saw her again; and the poetry, in retrospect, was naive, raw and embarrassingly laden with the obvious influence of some of those songwriters.

However, the poetry was now in my life as fact and what eventually followed in the London years, saw a very tangible development in its formation, in that city. Inevitably there happened in London, another brief encounter: a girl who was to smoulder, in the background of my life for the next twenty-five-odd years; but the poetry making, and its reading, had taken on its own life prior to this and now was established as a life-long presence in its own right.

*****

One of my fellow poets makes reference to 'cathartic process in high emotional times', as one generator in her poetic process; it goes without saying, that owning characteristics of the perennial romantic, has also a definite advantage. I have no doubt that somewhere in this process, lies the genesis of many a poet ... if not most. Once encountered, the joy of the process itself takes over; and who has never experienced the immediacy of the need to respond to the late-night visit from the muse, before chancing that unattended line or phrase, to dissolution in the morning light?

Another of my peers, echoes a core belief of mine, that "poetry should be read aloud". This may seem obvious but not necessarily so, by the evidence one sometimes encounters, masquerading as 'poetry'. The breaking-up of a piece of personal diatribe, a shopping list or even ordinary prose, into lines, no matter how creative on paper the arrangement may be, will rarely of itself, convincingly succeed as a credible poem; whilst unconstrained diatribe, however noble the cause, remains just that.

Conversely, some of our best prose, in itself contains more poetry than many 'poets' could ever hope to embody. Wherever one's poetic leanings lie, the acid test comes with an aural rendering of the work; and the line of distinction can often be tenuous, even arguable, as performance artists manage to make that shopping list or telephone directory resound with high drama.

Whatever the content or aim of a poem, it is in the words chosen and, most-importantly, the ordering of those words, irrespective of the simplicity or erudition of the language used, that the magic which sets it apart from its fellows, happens. There is a music with its own rhythm created; and like music, that rhythm and its key, can be regular or broken. Dylan Thomas relates that he wanted to write poetry in the beginning because he had fallen in love with words: it was the shapes and sounds of words, their music and colours, first heard from childhood, that he cared for; long before he learnt their meanings ... and this is evident in the lyric magic of the English language which pervades not only his poetry, but in like fashion, his prose.

The core energy of most creative endeavour resides in the process, the journey itself; rather than the product, the destination. It is the strength of this involvement, irrespective of its outcomes, which drives us to create. A satisfying outcome naturally provides the fertile ground for further endeavour but it remains the medium, rather than its manifestation, which ultimately provides us with the true creative impulse.

I am reminded of a discourse by Robert Graves from his 'Observations on Poetry 1922 - 1925', in which he states, "The nucleus of every poem worthy of the name is rhythmically formed in the poet's mind, during a trance-like suspension of his normal habits of thought ... learns to induce the trance in self-protection whenever he feels unable to resolve an emotional conflict by simple logic. If interrupted during this ... he will experience the disagreeable sensation of a sleep-walker disturbed; and if able to continue until the draft is completed, will presently come to himself and wonder: was the writer really he?" This is invariably what I feel ... where did that come from; how did I do that; did I do that?

There is always a sense of wonder, particularly in the wake of some very spontaneous poems, that they must have arrived from someplace outside of oneself.

*****

We now find ourselves living in this age of digital evolution/revolution and with it, have come times of unprecedented diversity in every aspect of the arts. The cleverness of the digital tool-bag, coupled with the immediacy of communications available to one and all, has provided the means for an unbounded level of creativity in most art forms to the point where almost anyone of a mind to do so, can and does call himself or herself, artist; and a world-class or award-winning one at that; while the true legitimacy of such qualification is seldom, if ever, questioned.

This no-holds-barred approach presents a bewildering array of choices in deciding what might, or might not, be regarded as art of true substance. In the minds of many, the digital tool seems to have become the end in itself: never mind the quality, feel the width; and the true skill of the artist himself or herself often appears derived from and dependent on, the medium itself. Perhaps it matters not, whether personal skill even exists at this high-point of the consumer age, where the packaging continues to be more important than the contents.

Inevitably, those who best take what they do most-seriously, tend to do so apart from the mainstream and with no thought of acceptance or otherwise, by the mainstream. The truth is, this is probably how it has always been; it is just that the mainstream has now swelled to a torrent, chattering and clamouring for recognition from its vast, ether-sustained audience. The old adage, where beauty resides in the eye of the beholder, hearer or reader, seems to verify the legitimacy of 'anything-goes' more than ever before, in these times of self-proclaimed greatness and mutual congratulation. Thankfully, there does remain an insistence and certainty for some, that there ultimately is an intangible quality which separates the gold from the dross; which elevates some expressions in every medium above most others: above the label of 'art' to that of significant, enduring Art.

In the final count, these truly-inspired creations identify themselves without the intervention of self-declaration or promotion but rather, by enduring in every culture, over time and circumstance: to survive the short-term lifespan of most objects in our current throw-away culture is a goal to which many may aspire but few realize.

This remains as true for poetry as for any of the art forms; and forms abound as never before. Style-camps in poetry undoubtedly do exist, often accompanied by a spirit of elitism which tends to exclude all other forms; and yet, it is not a matter of free-verse moderns verses rhyming-verse traditionalists, or any other 'style' camps. From past to present, there are as many interpretations of what constitutes poetry as there are poets: from the 'now-moment' brevity of a Japanese haiku to the epic story-telling of a Renaissance poet, where a single poem may run to volumes composed over many years; from the ballad of a bush poet to the accident of a 'found poem'; the legitimacy of each lies not in the selected poetic form but in the effectiveness of the poem's expression, outside of form.

A poem cannot help but be a personal expression, whether that be of one's own life, the observation of others lives, or of life and nature's many aspects; it reflects some emotional response to these things and as such, will always find a kindred soul with whom to resonate. Graffiti is also a personal expression and some, could even be said to rise to the elevated level of art; most, however, remains just angry or bored defacement in the public domain. So likewise, remains the personal diatribe or shopping list, randomly dissembled, no matter how much its author may declare it to be poetry. Unless it says something more, and in its manner of organization, lifts it out of mundanity and in its telling, works real magic.

* * * * *

And on the subject of graffiti, I now have the temerity to adorn this anthology with modest examples of my own. As someone whose professional working life has been devoted to the practice of architecture, and that, primarily in the role of design architect, it is natural that I should have had some continuing interest in drawing and related pursuits.

It was an early interest in drawing in a somewhat undirected way, in my primary school years, coupled with the suggestion of a vocational guidance officer (based on one of the tests, relating to three-dimensional visualization abilities), which led me to my initial impetus to pursue architecture as a suitable career. From that suggestion, flowed the choice of secondary school subjects, and even the choice of secondary school; amongst those subjects were technical drawing and art. Art, I enjoyed, but when I review my efforts from those years, I truly find nothing remarkable. This is probably still the case. However, I find that I have always had a modicum of natural ability which, even when neglected for years, never completely abandons me; and I do always enjoy it so much, when I rediscover it.

During my years in London, I discovered the joys of fine printmaking, specifically in the fields of serigraphy (screenprinting) and etching; with occasionally, a brief foray into monoprints. I continued this acquaintance for some time, on my return to Australia and should have done more. Life intervened and I lost that thread for some time. Latterly, having had one dear friend in an oils painting artist for many years until his death; and more recently another, as teacher and friend until his untimely death some years ago now, also in oil painting; I have, lazily I admit, been intent on painting in oils myself ever since. Amongst these pursuits, one consistent artistic thread has run through life: in the discipline of drawing, in various media. I enjoy drawing, be it in pencil, ink, charcoal, graphite; pen, quill, sharpened stick, bamboo pen, limp signwriter's brush: whatever can make a mark; and if it challenges the making of a mark, so much the better.

The images selected to punctuate these pages, have been taken from various sources; mostly produced over the timeline during which, the poems were composed – not absolutely so, however. Some may find their way in from earlier times, notably during university years; nor will they necessarily serve the same space in time, that a particular poem occupies. They are certainly not intended to illustrate particular poems; simply to accompany them. The media used, likewise will vary and generally be noted with the image; a small number of images will be taken from etchings or serigraph originals in colour; in the main, they will have come from drawing media already noted. I have enjoyed their production and I trust the reader may derive some enjoyment from their inclusions in my text.

Brad Drew

12th October 2015

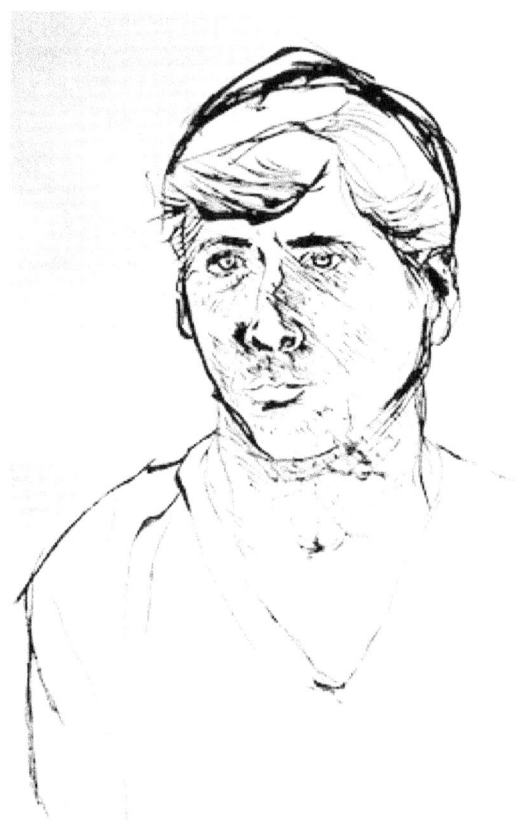

'Self Portrait 1983': Quill liner & indian ink on Fabriano paper

CONTENTS

FOREWORD:
INTRODUCTION:

THE POEMS:
LONDON 1974 TO 1977

SOUTHBANK BLUES: For Bernard   23

PUTNEY BRIDGE   24

POSTSCRIPT: 25

NEW YEAR 1976   27

PROCESSION   28
SYLVIE   28

DAWN HAIKU   29
STREET HAIKU   29

SPRING TANKA   30

SUNDAY TANKA   31

THE COACHMAN   33

PASTORALE   34

TANKA ON THE DAWN BEHIND YOUR DEPARTURE   35

YOU HAVE NOT CHANGED   37

WAKING POEM   38
GUINEVERE'S TANKA   38
COMPUTERIZED SONATA   38

POEM FOR RON   39
DID YOU EVER CRY?   39

HOLLOW HAIKU   40

THE KEEPER   41

LONDON SPRING   43
IN MY ASYLUM   43

COLUMBUS   44
REAP THE MARCH WINDS   44

WAKING POEM 2   45
SUNDAY TUBE TO PUTNEY BRIDGE   45

NONE OTHER ... EVER   46

TRAIN   47

POST-LONDON
BRISBANE MAY 2001 TO JUNE 2003

THE FISHER SWAIN   53

ANTELOPE DREAMS   59
COUPLING TANKAS: ON WAKING   59

REPRISE   60

MORNING SONG   61

THIRTY FIVE TANKAS OF LOSS AND DESOLATION ...
ONE TO FIVE : 24 May 2001   63

SIX TO TEN : 25 May 2001   64

ELEVEN TO FIFTEEN : 25 May 2001   65

SIXTEEN TO TWENTY : 26 May 2001   67

TWENTY-ONE TO TWENTY-FIVE : 26 May 2001   68

TWENTY-SIX TO THIRTY : 27 May 2001   69

THIRTY-ONE TO THIRTY-FIVE : 27 and 28 May 2001   70

MY BOAT UNDER THE STARS   71

ENLIGHTENMENT TANKAS   73

TO THE GODDESS WITHIN   74

REALTIME REVISITED 76

JACK 77

AND YET THEY THANK HER 79

I HAD WONDERED 81

TANKAS: REQUIEM FOR A GODDESS 83

BLACKALL RANGE
JULY 2003 TO THE PRESENT

PAGES 87

MOONSHINE ALLEY 88

DOWNPOUR IN THE CITY 90

AND IF I WERE ... 93

AS GRIEF'S FOR LOSS ... 94

SUMMER HAIKU, MT NEBO 96

MAPLETON DAWN 97
FINGAL, FEBRUARY 2004 97

AUTUMN TANKA 98
A SONG OF YEARNING 98

CONTRAST THIS WAVE 99

IN THE AFTERMATH 101

A PLAY ON PLAY 105
ON RAINY AFTERNOONS 105

GEISHA TANKA 106

IT CAME UPON A MIDNIGHT CLEAR 107

TIME SLIPS THE WARP 111

MUTE CELLS CRY OUT   112

WHAT CAUSED THE STATESMEN ALL   113

RETRIEVAL FRAGMENT   114

REVISITING'S A TURNING IN THE MIND   115
DUSK HAIKU   115

FOR MAURIE   117

HOW DEFTLY RUN   118
HAIKU ON RISING   118

THE DAY AFTER HAIKU   119
HOW CAME WE TO THIS DARKNESS?   119

A FENG SHUI CLEARING   121

TWIN EAGLES RISE   122

SONG FOR A FLAT WORLD   123

ANOTHER SONG OF SONGS :
CANTO I   124

CANTO II   126

CANTO III   129

CANTO IV   130

CANTO V   132
CANTO VI   132

CANTO VII   134

CANTO VIII   136

YOU ARE MY SONG   139

I THINK YOU HAVE, MY HEAD UNDONE   140

UPON THE NEW WORLD LANDFALL   141

A POEM FOR VALENTINE   142

THREE YEARS OUT   143

A POEM FOR CHRISTMAS   145

AND OF CONTENTMENT ...   146

FOUR YEARS HAVE COME TO US   147

ONE SEASON'S MOULD   148

MUTE SUNFLOWERS FROM GREY ASHES   149

AS AUTUMN TURNS ...   151

A SONNET FOR VALENTINE'S   152

TO LATER FRIENDSHIPS   153

A POEM FOR JULY   155

THREE NINDERRY TANKAS   156

'Jean Moreau': Pencil & mixed media on Ingres paper, 1976

LONDON:
APRIL 1974 TO MAY 1977

'The Berne Suit – Worb': Screenprint on Arches Dessin paper, 1981

'The Embankment': Rollerball & wash on Arches, 2015

SOUTHBANK BLUES: For Bernard

I had a friend here once, who loved this girl too well –
but never really should have:
because one day, she went out and married
someone else.
This much established, we went to a concert;
listened to some dancers, who periodically slipped
over a large banana, which the SM had thoughtfully written,
like the keystone of a silent movie,
on centre-stage, stage-left –
for the customers' enjoyment: in lieu of winter's frozen pools,
for fools, on busy pavements.

Intermission – twenty minute Southbank bar-rush:
beers, martinis, plastic cups –
ruminated both, on loves, who might have been;
had been, but weren't;
watched a surging sea of pretty breasts, pert asses:
flowed about us, like so many adolescent dreams;
and started,
at faces, that were almost faces we had known.
Much later,
walking on the rivered lights, back to The Embankment,
we declined a final drink, because
it was a long Tube home –
and cold.

PUTNEY BRIDGE

I loved you –
Oh! So well, that summer – and tonight,
a girl stood by me,
in rain on Putney Bridge, waiting
for a bus and looking,
so very much, like you.

I almost answered her eye –
only, she may not have been you;
and of that, I was afraid.

I stood with your phantom,
in two years' rain
and that last summer's dim traffic glow,
letting first one bus
and then another,
go lumbering on;
waiting to follow your memory,
just a little further.

I sit here still –
on an empty bus, in an empty London night,
while tears of rain
sweep moist-lidded windows; weep
a monsoon of memories,
of one still summer's night –

abandoned
to the damp embrace, of a steamy bus,
in the hissing kiss of wet tires –

and Cloverdale Park Nursery, seems so very far away.

'Spring Hill Street': Rapidograph on cartridge paper, 1966

POSTSCRIPT:

Remembering that something
never was –
Searching that something
never is –
Half-day removed –
still there and starting at visions,
in rain-spattered streets.

'My Great Grandparents, Robert & Elizabeth Higgenson':
Graphite block on cartridge paper, 2014

NEW YEAR 1976

I sit alone tonight –
waiting;
waiting in solemn ceremony;
waiting to take nineteen-seventy-six down
from its cardboard, top-of-cupboard prison:
waiting for the day of its parole,
these past two months.

I sit alone tonight –
waiting;
waiting for someone to come and say:
Hey! It's New Year's and you sit here alone,
waiting to let that silly box, down off the shelf;
down to let next year run loose?
Come out and have a drink!

Only I don't hear
anyone coming.

'Longing': Rollerball & wash on Arches paper, 2006

PROCESSION

Processions of days rush by, in an endless sweep
Of prehistoric wings, fabricated in memories
        of progression &
        regression –
It's March again & almost spring:
        smiles &
        flattering attentions –
      and everything is beautiful.

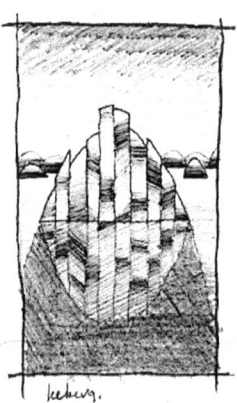

Notebook pencil study for 'Iceberg' print : 1979

SYLVIE

At least it's a luck
you don't close your windows –
it's not more than two hours,
I would have had to wait
behind a door!
I go home and come back
with your salad,
at around eight!

DAWN HAIKU

Amber-crisp dawning:
Dragonfly passes on sails,
Gossamer-woven.

'Dragonfly': Rollerball & wash on Arches paper, 2007

STREET HAIKU

Shaven heads, painted;
Finger-slapping brazen discs;
Handing out incense.

SPRING TANKA

Golden-skinned lovers,
Garlanded with beads of light,
Licking dawn's warm breath
On moistly-sweet tongues of night –
These perfect first daffodils.

'Daffodils': Rollerball & wash on Arches paper, 2007

SUNDAY TANKA

How gently there hangs
And quietly drops, the soft
Of this spring twilight –
Mingling and lost in your eyes,
Touched by the warmth of your smile.

'Head of a Girl': Rollerball & wash on Arches paper, 2007

'Bridge of Sighs, Venice': Screenprint on Arches Dessin paper, 1983

THE COACHMAN

Timeless dusk
and faceless breath of vast intrigue,
who guide with easy hand, this coach:
take me –
willing guest and passenger of endless dawn,
I'll ride beside your presence,
trusting and keeping
the smells of each new sunrise, that you bring.

'Seaside Platter': Rollerball & wash on Arches paper, 2006

PASTORALE

Nestled by your side,
I watched you sleeping –
And fields of poppies
Broke across your cheeks;
Your smile rose up
And, draped with pearls,
Stepped out to dance among them.

'Bumblebee': Rollerball & wash on Arches paper, 2006

TANKA ON THE DAWN BEHIND YOUR DEPARTURE ON WINGS, NOT SO DARK, AS KEPT IN SECRET TRUST

What might be written,
When the sun has extinguished
And dimmed this fresh world?
Wait! It is only eclipsed –
Behind the moon, it burns still.

'Study for St Marks': Pastel on cartridge paper, 1981

'A Friend of My Grandfather from WW1':
Conte crayon on cartridge paper, 2013

YOU HAVE NOT CHANGED

You have not changed –
And winds that bore you from me,
like sails of neon men-of-war, full-thrust
against past tides of cities: lit with efflorescent lens
of dew and time-shined spores;
have kept you –
I, the wind-maker.

You have not changed –
And I, the firefly and moth
of constant dreams and surging sands: these fluxing tides
of shifting, in the glow of ancient keeps, built high
on wave-strewn coastlines;
have kept you –
I, the wind-maker.

You have not changed –
And clouds that bore you in me,
light as dusk, on distant forms of stream-swept jade;
down sweet banks, on polished sleds of glass,
fresh-cut from Chartres' ancient rose;
have kept you –
I, the born-on-wind.

You have not changed –
And youthful blooms of forest depths,
light with their fires,
the phoenix keep: fanned high
by winds that bore you to me;
sails that kept you –
You, the wind-rider.

WAKING POEM

Seven a.m. – and a jet just swam
across my morning sunbath,
wiping its shadow over my face:
a washer-full of last week's words,
scribbled on a subway wall.

GUINEVERE'S TANKA

Cassidy's is the
World's first, patented timelock:
Braving tall seas on
Sails, fashioned from the plankton
Of Camelot's silent sighs.

'Torso': Sharpened stick & ink on rusted Arches paper, 2006

COMPUTERIZED SONATA

I am taking an inventory of your body
          with a digital IBM:
It's a delicate process
& could   take   a   long   time.

POEM FOR RON

Another morning at the office
as he sits behind me, marching on that apple –
advancing over it:
like treading the forgotten bones
of a long-lost general, at dawn,
on plains of ancient Babylon.

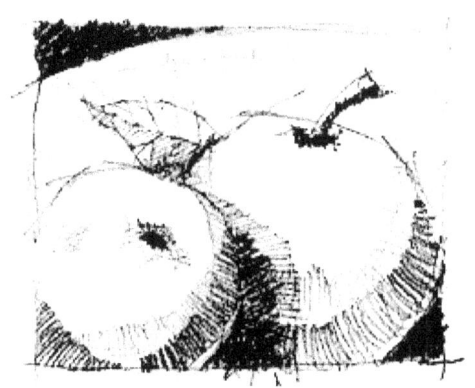

'Apples': Pencil on Arches paper, 2006

DID YOU EVER CRY?

Do not fear for
The sweet, sibilant whispers
Of the rustling leaves
Of sorrow –
For sighing sings the softest
Of the sibyl's songs.

HOLLOW HAIKU

Springtime love affairs
Should claim only the stout heart –
It's summer again.

'Seated Woman': Sharp stick with ink on cartridge paper, 2009

THE KEEPER

The keeper is lost –
And losing, so the unsheathed ring:
Time's annulary, bared in solemn gambit,
Gambled for an unseen queen –
She rings the pealing
Of the hours and houri, measured out upon
The bane Achilles held –
She keeps, and holding,
Holds his unkeeped heart
And bares it to the light of day.

The keeper is lost –
And keeping, keeps his solaced keep:
Kept high on castled crags, between the distance
Of his bursting soul's intent –
In his watch-housed sleep,
He's marked her measures;
Timed her hours of queen-shod waking –
For the outlawed swain, Astarte weep:
For he's pawned his heart
And bears it from the light of day.

*Written originally in London 1975 and, as fate would have it,
a prologue to 'The Fisher Swain', some twenty-five years,
and half a world later, in Brisbane.*

'Grail' : Rollerball & wash on Arches paper

*'St Mark's, Venice': Felt marker on tracing paper –
Stencil master for screenprint, 1981*

LONDON SPRING

The lissom curving of your spine
    Reminds me of antelopes
        In a sun-swept day –
So, often-times,
I walk behind you.

'Rain Music': Rollerball, wash & correction pen on Arches paper, 2006

IN MY ASYLUM

You see:
I have this crazy impulse to follow
every woman who looks vaguely like you.
You could be leading me home.

There,
every taxi's door, sounds like your footstep.
Consequently, I make a lot of false starts –
like a blind sprinter, on an empty track.

COLUMBUS

I played in the bath
With your rubber duck, last night;
Pretending you were there,
With chrome-plate wings,
Waiting to return it, like Columbus –
Sailing from the New World,
Under fair skies and the gentle hint
Of dusk,
Between the valley of your thighs.

'Shells': Rollerball & wash on Arches paper, 2006

REAP THE MARCH WINDS

Reap the March winds
for a few days' madness –
steal the dead of night
from the Blind King's purse
and, singing in the madhouse heat,
reach out –
for she'll never come this way
again.

WAKING POEM 2

Night's ghost flees misted window panes,
fire glowing, growing in the grate –
lone shaft of wintered sunlight
strokes window jamb and falteringly,
feels its way across the room.

'Gordon Place Fireplace': Quill & Ink on Arches paper, 2007

SUNDAY TUBE TO PUTNEY BRIDGE

My hands are shaking today
Because I've had too much coffee
And not enough black sleep –
Or, was it coming to see you?

NONE OTHER ... EVER

You walked my way
And drew warm vapours of scented fields
Across my sight.
You rose to greet me
And in so doing, loosed a thousand
Shimmering jewels
From your lips.

You brought this day,
Deep in your pocket,
To show only me,
In the stillness of night.

You stirred in my world
And the hint of your movement
Sent rainbow-blessed insects
From flickering leaves,
Rising and soaring
To welcome your light.

'Torso': Bamboo pen & ink on rusted Arches Paper, 2006

TRAIN:
EIGHT-THIRTY PADDINGTON TO PLYMOUTH

Eight-thirty train to Exeter –
Two hours and forty minutes:
Reading-Taunton-Exeter St Davids –
           What's Plymouth?

England slipping by in nameless haze,
As the Inter-City knife-slice
Pulses:: Throbs:: and Penetrates:: in
Lengthy intercourse on Devon fields;
And holdings, cottages and barns,
Hedgerows, fences, stiles and downs:
Struggling greenery trying hard,
           These waterways and trees –

Pulses:: Throbbing::
Coursing down the thighs of Noble England:
Grey, grey blankets draped,
Draped in loose, soiled folds caressing,
Clinging these recumbent loins –
           Ecstasy of the Eight-thirty
           Paddington-to-Plymouth.

Second lunge-thrust of the day,
Slipping smoothly down, day-long –
           Coming:: Coming::
           Oh! I'm coming!
Rape of England!

LIBS THROW A SPANNER, read the headlines.
On her back and I'm here, languishing
           In Inter-City come.
Black-faced sheep, cottages and rolling fields,
           Forever –

Ah! A junkyard!
Scrapped and beat-up, dented, battered,
Rusted, rotting cars: How quaint!
   Where's spring?
   And where are you,
   My Love?

Trees burning –
Burning-out, on sheltered side
Of hill, and Mother's home; and
Children playing at her knees:
Tends the kitchen,
Keeps the home fires burning –
And Father's burning tree stumps
    On the hill.

Embers glow in mist-swathed morning,
Lunch approaching, Father's coming,
   All is well –
   And England lives.

Spring coming:: Blankets hugging::
British Rail's swollen member throbs;
Throbs on through the South-West,
   Under blankets,
Dirtied with its countless comes.
   Wasn't it good,
   My Love? My Loves?

You, whom I loved, and love –
I bear you with me, as we make it::
Sigh and make it:: Sigh and brake it::
   Braking it:: In Taunton::

Spread-out under milky skies,
Stretched from star to star,
   There:: Here::
We were frozen:: there:: forever –
In moments:: that were::
   Before they:: That are –

And I am locked here:: now::
As I have been:: Will be –
Thudding:: Pounding:: Throbbing:: Pulsing::
Post-Taunton Blues – Oh God!
        I'm coming!
        Tadpole legionnaire:
I've closed the ranks.
St David's discharge and I'm gone –
Just another spunky frog,
        Lost-in-action,
        Exeter,
Thirty-first of March, Nineteen Seventy-seven.

Written during a morning rail journey to Exeter, on office business,
having recently read Allen Ginsberg's lengthy poem, 'Iron Horse';
inspired by, rather than emulating, that work.

'Landscape with Hills': Etching on zinc plate, 1976

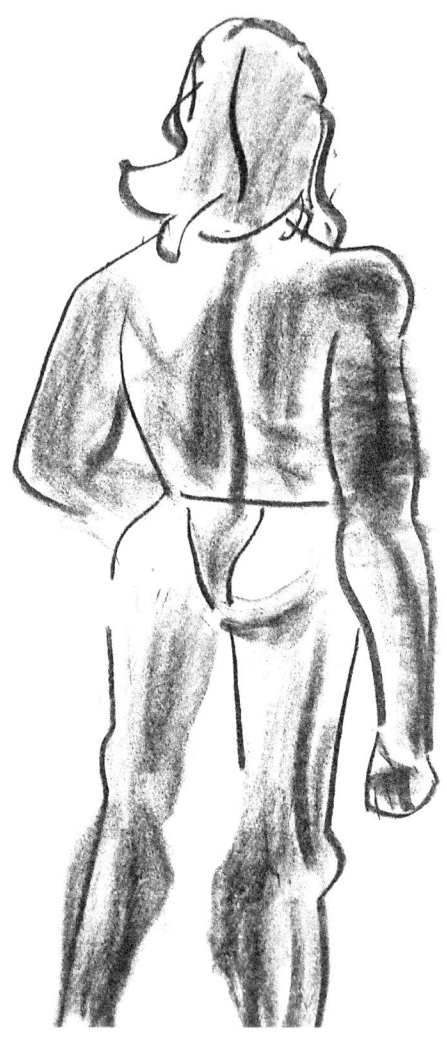

'Norman': Compressed charcoal on newsprint, 1966

POST-LONDON:
BRISBANE MAY 2001 TO JUNE 2003

'Frank & Lilly': Compressed charcoal on newsprint, 2002

'Grail Image': Rollerball & wash on Arches paper, 2014

THE FISHER SWAIN

Exiled heart and outlawed swain –
each night: a year – he dreamt in vain;
dreamt of longing and desire,
each night: a year –
each day: a fire.
Seven, and-one-half, millennia
thus, he dreamt, the Keeper-lost:
so great the cost
of unseen queen and all she meant –
and so, he dreamt.

   Astarte wept –

For his pawned heart, wept – and weeping,
hid it from the light of day.
Distanced, bursting soul's intent:
the queen-shod, nightly pealing rent
one heart in two;
kept one half and all its healing –
Bell-keeper and Time's broker,
bearer of Fate's annulary,
bared in silence long ago:
solemn gambit, unseen queen.

   Astarte wept –

Whose the tolling; whom the weeping;
whose the dreaming; whom the sleeping?
Distanced in his bursting soul, he slept
and dreamt – and dreaming, dreamt
of being lost and all it cost.

   Sleeping thus, he dreamt again –

Hours and houri lost to sight,
years sweep by in endless flight;
the beat of wings drown out his plight –
their beating lulls his sleep at night,
quells his dreams, his quest for life.
To still the throngs who storm his gates
Penelope-like, he undertakes
to knit a shawl, a home, a cairn –
and knitting thus, some action make,
to quench this thirst, which will not slake.

   And once, he dreamt –

Waking, dreamt he saw her yet;
knew that he could not forget
her face, her form, her inner light –
her sight and sound, that burned so bright
and burning, put his soul to flight,
forever owning all his nights.

   Astarte slept –

Sleeping thus, his heart, she kept.
Of purpose lost, of fire bereft,
he put away his joys and slept;
wounded with a toxin deep,
he sought some solace in his sleep.
Queen-shod pealing in the night;
grail-quest fire that burned so bright –
wound complete, he saw her yet;
wondered then, would she forget
one brief, one flaring light.

Astarte slept –

Eternity, he dreams and sleeps –
sweet sleep: an opiate to his days.
He knits his shawl and seeks a way
to find some meaning to his fate:
the wound he would, if could, negate.
Another place, he saw the gleam –
tried to forget what might have been;
to put away, both soul and mind
believing that, with friends and time:
distractions of another kind –

his wound would heal and slowly bind.

The world he sought, whilst mostly good,
had not the test of time withstood:
the rigours of a heart bereft.
The friends he gained, pained for his plight
and heard his emptiness at night –
besieged by calls of night-shod queen,
core of whom, he once had been:
the span of which, however slight,
he'd been her passion for one night –
or two, or three, or more?

He'd made no count; he'd kept no score –

It had not really mattered then.
Could it have been thus, truly been,
little more than just a dream:
illusion of a heart, grown sore –
an apparition, once he'd seen?

In constancy, Astarte slept –

And sleeping still, she gave no sign;
no word of queen or how, her life.
If only once for him, she'd called
and gave a purpose to his shawl,
his shroud: for thus it seemed.

Bereft of purpose and of queen,
he hid in darkness, growing dim:
apothecary's dream.
But still, forlorn Astarte slept,
while swain, cleft from his dreams, bereft –

   pondered queen; her life –

Her life, he'd never questioned – for,
with beauty, and the joys she brought,
could not come pain, with burden fraught.
How could she suffer, ever bright,
when love and beauty were her right?
In reading now, his last refrain
from long ago – a poem called Train –
he shakes with dawning and alarm:
perhaps was he, had done her harm;
had left an accidental scar,

   she carried with her from afar –

that onetime, sometime, distant past,
he loved, and had been loved, by her.
Could something there, have led her feet
to flee to Devon, in retreat?
Or was the verse, mere prophesy
of chance, but nothing more?

   Astarte stirs –

Foolish swain, Astarte chides –
that you might ponder so, you're dreaming:
that you, with her, could leave some meaning;
lead her, somehow, to that place;
leave her, in a state of grace –
longing likewise, for your face?

You're mad! It's nothing more, than fate!

But what if, more than poem-forsook,
it led her, to the course, she took?
And coursing so, you would not know –
you thought her gone: another's queen;
her destiny and yours, unseen.
You would have followed, had it been.

Astarte wakes –

What is her wound, this Fisher Queen?
What hurt, what pain, what sorrow: spleen?
He senses it and feels the ill:
the malady she suffers, still.
She flees in terror and alarm,
afraid that he, might do her, harm.
What harm was done, he cannot know –
and so, he curses mind, so slow:
so thick – that he might never grasp,
the depth or meaning, of his task.

Astarte wakes and rises –

What if the cup they seek, were one:
both wounds, to share and overcome;
in constancy, their hurts, to spare;
in loving and with caring, where
one grail, for both, becomes.
Astarte placed grails in two hearts:
hiding them in distant parts;
waiting for the time to come,
when destiny would make as one,
a product greater, than its sum.

Seven, and-one-half, millennia of exile –

Was she there, for him to find?
Or was she only in his mind?
Was it always meant that way:
the swain, to wander every day;
and through each night, pursue his plight –
her being, always in his sight:

  her sound, his soul?

> *A conclusion, of sorts, some twenty-five years later, to The Keeper,*
> *written in London, in 1975: a conclusion which was to remain,*
> *forever un-concluded, suspended in what Japanese Ukio-e artists*
> *would call, 'the floating world'.*

'Standing Figure': Compressed charcoal on cartridge paper, 2009

ANTELOPE DREAMS

Once again,
antelope dreams abound –
They fill my nights and days, with longing
for sun-swept plains and the soft,
sweet scent of you.

Once again,
I hunger but to hear your sound:
the drumming of their hoofs to drown
and feast my eyes, with the ever-lissom
curving of your spine.

How can I sleep at all –
Again, still, or ever?
I can only watch in thrall
and walk behind you.

A reprise of sorts, to 'London Spring', some 25 years earlier

COUPLING TANKAS: ON WAKING

For, were I to gaze
upon you every day –
new longing would stir
me afresh, with each sunrise,
resting spoon-wise by your side.

For, were I to wake,
sated with last night's loving –
resting by your side,
head, heart and loins would quicken
to the touch and smell of you.

And, were I to write
these verses every night,
upon your fair skin –
visions of your morning form
would urge their soft retelling.

REPRISE

With those first words,
You cleared these ears of deafness –
And forgotten yearnings stirred,
Of dreams, in nights so endless.

With that first kiss,
You woke this heart from sleeping,
Through remembered longing's mists,
Which kept you in their keeping.

With that first, later coupling,
You balmed these limbs in sweetness –
Peeled back the years of suffering
And bathed with love so selfless.

With kisses, words and loving,
You've corrected this life's list –
Returned the song, so long unheard;
Reclaimed for me, the joys forsaken;
Restored to me, the path once taken.

So long ago, you claimed this heart –
If claim is made, it's yours.
You've had it from the start.

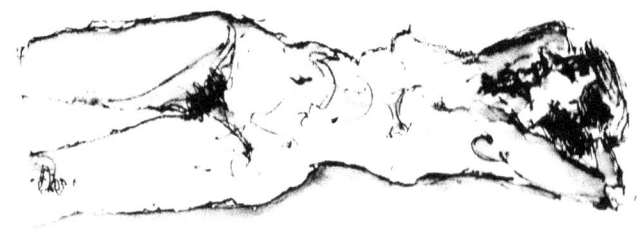

'Reclining Figure': Rollerball & wash on Arches paper 2007

MORNING SONG

Quicksilver morning,
sliding over treetops;
gut-wrenching longing,
holds me pinned against
these walls, sans toi.
Freshly-pressed, a Jarrett phrase
caresses face with tears:
a gentle waterfall to splash
softly, past agony's rocks –
while fresh-drawn coffee
steams, with a dash.

Quicksilver mourning:
my cough matches yours;
matches yours, my fate.
Mercureal rising –
pined against my walls,
I cough, and reach
for another cigarette;
toi-bound, sky-bound,
thigh-bound, unbound:
The Almighty Key
to all the others.

'Figure': Rollerball & wash on Arches paper, 2007

'Standing Woman': Compressed charcoal on cartridge paper, 2007

THIRTY-FIVE TANKAS OF LOSS AND DESOLATION …

ONE TO FIVE : 24 May 2001

A cold wind blowing,
Words and birds drop from branches –
Winter already?
Empty branches break like hearts
And spring will not come again.

Chill descends on heart –
Brel accompanies it now
And limbs grow restless.
Was it only yesterday
When love, at last seemed so real?

Autumn was so short –
Can that be snow already,
When leaves are still gold?
Just an early frost, swept down
From heights of aspiration.

The gods must laugh now,
At such insolence: that she
Could love him, only.
Listen, while his heart breaks like
Empty branches in winter.

Brel still fills his ears –
The night is long and empty;
Winter hounds his door.
Summer and autumn are gone;
Winter chills his aching heart.

SIX TO TEN : 25 May 2001

Icy wind beats door –
Lights flicker, then extinguish;
Only wind remains.
Was autumn so late coming,
That winter is here so soon?

A fallen flower?
No, just a crushed butterfly –
Someone held it close.
Insects are such fragile things;
Sit still and let them alight.

Lone bird drops from sky;
A sharp crack breaks the silence –
The last hunter's gun?
No, a branch heavy with snow
And sound of one heart breaking.

Shaking, outstretched hand;
A crumpled piece of colour –
Someone's used Kleenex?
Love's quivering butterfly
Should not be held so closely.

A muffled retort –
Love's suicide smokes gently
And crumpled soul flees:
One poet spoke too freely
And singed the wings of freedom.

ELEVEN TO FIFTEEN : 25 May 2001

This blood heat plummets,
Body racked with shivering –
But winter in May?
The foot-shot poet shudders,
As love and life seep from him.

One foot in bucket,
He limps across the room; and
Memories of mouth.
The poet's songs fell lifeless
At the alter of his love.

This night is so cold,
His bones and heart cry to him:
Where is his love's fire?
This has promise of being
A long and empty winter.

Why love's suicide
Must be inevitable,
The heart cannot tell –
Butterflies lie quivering,
As evidence of clutching.

A path of Kleenex!
A great lover has walked here:
This is evidence!
So many crushed butterflies
Testify his way with words.

'My Grandmother, Emma Lavina Ashby':
Compressed charcoal on cartridge paper, 2014

SIXTEEN TO TWENTY : 26 May 2001

He recognizes
That he walked this path before:
Crushed wings litter it.
Don't clutch their wings but let them
Brush against you, when ready.

An empty churchyard –
No votive offering there,
For the suicide.
The poet took his own love
With too many miss-timed words.

They said: Don't worry –
She just needs a little space:
But he knew better.
Winter winds howled at his door
And torn wings seeped under it.

A heart lies open –
This is no operation
But a tragedy:
The poet opened his heart,
Then ground down his foot in it.

Oh, luckless poet!
To wait so long for summer,
To find it cancelled –
Verses fell from high above;
Past hurts turned them to snowflakes.

TWENTY-ONE TO TWENTY-FIVE : 26 May 2001

A bare, empty sky;
A bald rock and a barren tree;
A sharp, clear coldness –
Dirty smudge on horizon
Heralds a coming snowstorm.

In middle of night,
The poet calls out her name –
And the clock ticks on.
Winds of hurt muffle his cry
And terror covers her heart.

When it's winter here,
Half-world away, comes summer:
That's where she will be –
With her, comes summer and spring;
With him, comes only, the fall.

Fresh sheets are useless,
Whatever hopes may have been,
For an empty bed –
Just as useless, are sweet words,
To a heart that's torn by hurt.

Scent of butterflies,
Crushed by hasty affection,
Mingle with longing –
Unpacked sheets taunt the poet,
As midnight comes and passes.

TWENTY-SIX TO THIRTY : 27 May 2001

The door stands open –
He dare not nudge it, for fear
That no-one is there:
He saw the wild geese winging
And the onset of winter.

Unseasonal chill,
With unreasonable fear,
Freezes his movements –
He sees the littered corpses:
These quivering butterflies.

What day can this be?
Since butterfly message came,
He lost track of time –
Is this autumn or winter,
That litters the path, with wings?

Alan Watts and zen,
Haunt the poet's reasoning:
Of why, how and when –
When is love, if it's broken?
Why is hurt, how lovers fear?

The zen of loving
Turns all reason, upside down:
Makes fools of sages.
When is she, if she's loving?
Why is he, when she's hurting?

THIRTY-ONE TO THIRTY-FIVE : 27 and 28 May 2001

New moon and stillness
Ooze under this door's threshold,
Bringing heart-deep chill –
The forecast was for such joy
And suddenly, it's sleeting.

In another life,
Winter came this early, twice,
Without forewarning –
One would think, that he should learn
To pack woollies and warm vests.

From out of clear sky,
A small speck plummets earthward:
A meteorite?
Just a small starling, struck down
By winter's chill, of lost love.

Winter sun on back,
The poet shakes off ennui;
Turns his mind to spring –
The wild geese will then return,
Bringing joys, to light his nights.

Today is warmer:
A chrysalis is splitting,
Heralding the spring –
Metamorphosis complete,
Soft, crushed wings may yet unfurl.

MY BOAT UNDER THE STARS

My boat under the stars
Has become my favorite place.
It's there, with love's compass,
I can both charter time and space;
And when the moon is full,
Steer my craft by the light of your face:
Heaven's helmsman, full of grace.

My starboat's name is Ever –
You are its guiding light;
As aeons spin about me,
You maintain my course at night;
And when no stars prevail,
Provide a glow, however slight:
Heaven's highway, clear and bright.

'From Falconcourt': Rollerball & wash on Arches paper, 2012

'Lost Dog Gothic': Screenprint on Arches Dessin paper, 1982

ENLIGHTENMENT TANKAS

With these feet on ground,
With this head among the stars,
I am neophyte –
Hold me, stretched from pole to pole;
Centre my being with yours.

Abstraction resting
In a sky pregnant with stars:
Boundless universe –
Once touched, the soul is boundless;
All beliefs, wrested from this.

'Mushroom Vase': Rollerball & wash on Arches Paper, 2006

TO THE GODDESS WITHIN

Ancient seed of sleeping sky,
In vengeance, wrested from those thighs
Of father, by a Titan son:
Her sickle-handed sibling –
The goddess woke; and woke the world
To fearsomeness and beauty.
Deep from shell-strewn temple bounds,
She reigns and walks the world
In love and beauty awesome –
Thus walking, lives the goddess;
Wakes within us all.

* * * * *

I watch the walkers
And walking thus, watch I,
These margins of a surging realm,
Stretched wide between the shore and sky
In majesty and plumbless depths:
Mere edges of that consciousness.
I love this space, this interface
That stretches to the sky –
So, walking thus and watching thus,
Walk I.

I watch in wonder
And wondering thus, watch I,
The beauty of these fearsome depths:
Vast surgings of a consciousness,
Released upon our sphere of being
Men and gods, mere instruments
Of heaven's promptings, locked
In waking dreams and aspirations,
Suspended in the sky –
So, wondering thus and dreaming thus,
Watch I.

When you're withdrawn and at your ebb,
Your temple, lost in deepness,
Your sighing whispers:
"I am here. This is no web –
For I am resident, beyond the seagull's crying;
I am your body's element and bearer of your soul;
I am the yin, your feminine: the truth to make you whole.
I come in beauty, come in love: the content of your chalice –
The half you lost and laid aside, your very grist and core.
I shore your soul and shoring thus,
Your soul, in shoaling, soars."

'Susan's Shells': Rollerball & wash on Arches paper, 2006

REALTIME REVISITED

Realtime? Yes –
I heard it long ago and thought
it simply myth:
a childlike fable, danger-fraught:
a longing, that all good sense taught,
could be no more
than just a glyph.

Realtime? Yes –
I heard it ringing frequently
and thought it out of season;
of how it could not be,
but yet, it pealed incessantly,
defying ears to pause, to doubt
the gulf, which seemed so wide;
that time and years, seemed to divide –
yet realtime, will not hang about.

Realtime? Yes –
I've heard its passing, in my night
and wondered, if that footstep,
heard however slight,
might with my soul,
one day, take flight –
to be more than just gift.

'Lions of Venice': Pencil & ink on tracing film, 1983

JACK

My sprawling Jack-of-Frost
lays on his back – accosts
me, with the tune
that hangs me from him.
He tunes the song he sings,
with keepsakes, lacking strings
or sounding-boards
for yesterday's illusions.

My scornful Jack-of-Frost
swings from my back and scoffs
about the lack
of rhyme or reason.
He reasons, as he rants,
about the obstacles of chance –
a steeplechase
of falls, and fate's contusions.

My robbing Jack-of-Grief
steals across me, in my sleep,
to render down
the turgid fat of reason.
He renders, as he paints
from the palette, time acquaints
with weeping wounds
and destiny's deep lesions.

My distant Jack-of-Reason
slips inside me out of season
and spreads his tendrils
gently, through my spine.
He thrusts his fingers deep,
through the tissue of my sleep –
an alchemist
in animus confusions.

My whistling Jack-in-Season
rubs against me, with good reason,
as he modulates
the passage of the song.
His melody now falters,
as its tempo gently alters;
and it moves into a somewhat-minor key,
of changes, chords well-tempered,
diminished, but augmented –
the theme, its own, defying transposition.

Of all the Jacks-that-Gather
in these days, the one that matters
most of all, is that,
of mocking Jack-of-Truth:
that prince of lost illusions
and price of thought transfusions,
sees life – a leap of faith,
not wanting proof.

'Talisman Doll': Pencil on Arches paper, 2006

AND YET THEY THANK HER

Just another scalp, on the belt
of the goddess moving fleet-foot
through the undergrowth,
sliding through the shadows
of ghosts and summers past –
and, silent as the mists of morning,
melt and vanish in the cold
hard light of day.

Just another pelt, to charm
the waistline of a silent sylph
moving with a grace
that time forgot, but not
forgotten by the bald ones
listing in her wake –
no time could take from them
the hunger, she so readily begot.

And yet they thank her
for their baldness,
listing,
hunger –
beg her, once again
to charm their senses,
take their skin
and wear it, for her own.

'My Outlook': Chinese brush & rollerball on Arches paper, 2006

'Genet à Kemp': Monoprint on rice paper, 1981

I HAD WONDERED

I had wondered when you left,
If words would dry
Like leaves before their falling;
If like the thoughts,
Would tongue be cleft –
And left to flounder as some wreck,
Stranded on the shoals
Of summer's passage.

I have wondered with you gone,
If thoughts would fly
Like leaves at autumn's calling;
If with its call,
Would end our song –
As might migrate the noble swan,
Leaving at the first
Grey hint of winter.

I have wondered in your void,
If tongue would tie
Like bells bereft of tolling;
If in that lull,
Of peal devoid,
Few other means might be deployed
To warn of danger –
Save life's barge from shoaling.

For I have laboured in your wake,
My voice to fly; this thirst to slake;
The beast to name, that in my waking,
Hunts me in this undertaking –
Breathing down my neck and days,
Intent to rob from me that tune,
Hanging from my voice – consumed
By self-defeating torpor.

But I will yield no satisfaction,
For the beast thrives on inaction –
The roots and fruits, his thrusting snout
Grub out, are those of faith and doubt;
The faith to love, the doubt to leave:
Twin yarns in the magician's sleeve,
Best separated on the loom,
By reconfiguring fate's tune.

'Elephant Seals': Rollerball on Arches paper, 2006

TANKAS: REQUIEM FOR A GODDESS

Standing in the waste
Where scattered hearts lie fractured,
Gleaming at her feet;
The stage lies empty, soundless –
Footlights dimmed, the cast has left.

When all that is left
Is grey of autumn's dreaming,
What will it matter
How adoration flattered
When the gods and beauty fly?

A lonely runner
Pounds the life-long pavement course,
Running for her life;
For or from, is the question –
Is she chasing or fleeing?

'Clouds at Dusk': Rollerball & wash on Arches paper, 2006

'In a Corner of Venice': Screenprint on Arches Dessin paper, 1983

BLACKALL RANGE
JULY 2003 TO THE PRESENT

*'My Grandfather, Herbert Drew, 1915': Conte crayon
& compressed charcoal on cartridge paper, 2013*

PAGES

In the stillness
and the breaking of the night,
stars wink out and daylight hums,
to draw from sleep, put dreams to flight.
The book lies open – this day's life
awaiting substance from its source,
to draw from dreams, a present course.

Hordes throng the gates –
the audience is restless,
all tickets paid, the cast arrayed
in all their tatty splendour.
Both living and the dead cry out,
seek recognition from some doubts:
their meaning, cause, their tenure;
the mundane duties, must-be-dones,
the hopes, the dreams, the pleasures.

Aches and longings hang at bay,
aspirations pending –
the quest remains still, veiled in haze,
its story, never-ending.
Procrastination clouds the mind,
prevarication circling;
the clamour and the din increase –
Where's comprehension, bringing peace?

In the awkwardness
and finality of silence,
thoughts won't stop
and words won't come,
to still the brain's incessant hum.

MOONSHINE ALLEY

Almost moonshine alley,
and the clunking, bamboo clatter
of the wind-chime stills the air
that drives the scudding white caps
through the sky –

and hair that ruffles
in the madness, of the flight
down firefly highways,
with the words that none dare whisper
to the night.

Listing moonshine galley,
and staccato tree-frogs stammer,
as the wind-chime fills the air
that drives the scudding memories
from the sky –

and fear that scuffles
with the sadness, of the flight
of gadfly byways,
and the thoughts that come unbidden
to the night –

where thirsting memory mingles
with present tense: the sense
that all things started, and abandoned
to that flight, fell in a time
when all seemed ripe

and ready to the touch of discontent –
when beckoning firefly highways
gave way to gadfly byways
while meaningless distractions
drowned the air.

Almost moonshine alley,
and the cheerful bamboo chatter
of the wind-chime clears the air
that drives the scudding whitecaps
through the sky –

and hair that ruffles
in the gladness, of the flight
of firefly highways,
with the thoughts, that one dares whisper
to the night.

'From Bald Knob': Zinc plate etching on rag paper, 1980

DOWNPOUR IN THE CITY

Downpour in the city –
and the solitary rainspout, swells to overflowing,
spews its overburden, without discrimination:
cuts a swathe and parts the wave
of lemming-borne umbrellas,
beating their hasty crocodile retreat
from this sudden
and most unseasonable deluge.

Friday afternoon, and downpour in the city –
the drumming din drowns out the traffic roar,
the maitre d', all idle conversation.
Lovers huddle in sudden intimacy
along the café margins
and downwind of the deluge
trapped against the surging lemming tide
in abrupt, but not unwelcome, togetherness.

Hardly-hidden headlamps blazing
skinny girls light their way towards a virgin destiny
while grim-faced shoppers
Christmas-clutching one free arm
brave the tide and scuttle, in a rush none understands:
seasonal programming –
scuttle bugs wend and weave their tenuous way
and still, the solitary giant pisses on.

Accents jostle with the downpour din –
solemn matriarchs with spouse in tow
(imports from another place)
emerge in gentle bewilderment
intents for promenade, now foiled.
Large-nosed girls, small breasts and teasing eyes
aflame with matching egos, breast the tide
to dance the tourist tango.

This is glorious –
Buenos Aires must have been like this
when cafes thronged and spilled the streets
and sudden and unseasonable downpours
fed the urgency of life;
when poets and rebels mingled with the heady
sweaty smell of rushing Friday afternoons
pungent coffee, cigarettes, sudden rain and mobsters.

The cast and faces have not changed -
dark-suited businessmen, intent and sombre
feign ignorance of rain, intent upon their goals.
The timid girls with teasing eyes
dance and weave their breasting way
from an anonymous future;
while tourists and matrons, spouse atow
(parcel-packing first of season's shoppers)
brave the dance of Friday city flights
and still, the solitary giant pisses on.

'The Last Resort': Screenprint on Arches Dessin paper, 1983

'My Grandmother, Elizabeth Price Higgenson':
Conte crayon & charcoal on cartridge paper, 2013

AND IF I WERE ...

And if I were to take this tale,
Write it, such as gods might pale
In all their bland uncertainty,
That men may feel these things –

That centuries might claim their genes,
Fill them with recurring themes
Of madness and of vision –

Here, in seeming non-avail, I hover,
Life and love withstanding,
Lodged between the darkness
And the light.

'Alpine Village': Screenprint on Arches Dessin paper, 1982

AS GRIEF'S FOR LOSS …

As Grief's for loss, so Grief's a cross to bear
Through autumn's dreaming days, a course to share –
Thus dreaming, grieve the passing of the years
Of friends, of youth, the wellspring's hopes and fears;
'Til Grief herself, becomes too much to bear,
Engenders silence, thus to stem despair:
Suspend the fall, the plight of flailing nights
Which Grief bestows, on all whom she ignites.

Thus grieved we all, the silent mute: the wall
Pain raised about, as rampart to your fear –
Not for yourself, but for the ones held dear;
And silenced thus, a clotted, sanguine thrall
Plied hidden bindings; and with gag replete,
Enforced a stillness, as such griefs accrete –
Consigned to rest within a living tomb,
Endure faux death, in antiseptic gloom.

There, in the stillness, by such silence wrought,
Where sight and sound alone, accompany thought –
And gates are shut on all that might be said,
Where living bodies masquerade as dead;
Where well-meant smiles deny what might be real,
Unshielded words let slip, despite all zeal,
Taunt, torture, torment, slip the knot of hope –
Locked eyes, lashed ears, the bounds of your world's scope.

* * *

To languish not, between two worlds to hang,
But storm the ramparts of the blood, that sang
Your grief, to sleep the dream of no avail,
You summoned up your willpower, to prevail
And loose the bonds, which held you in their keep:
Turn back the flood which fevered sanguine sleep –
When grief alone, is all that's left to ply,
Some hope must filter through, to death decry.

To fade not, through insistent, failing night,
One spark alone, was all it took to fight –
Regain a hold, on all your joys held dear;
Turn back the flood of Grief, with purpose clear,
And garner up a host of precious hours –
But was it just for your joy, or for ours,
That time and tide retreated with those years,
In laughter, more than in the stead of tears?

Retreat they did, in part, but part alone,
As if the world in full, could not atone:
Wipe out each blemish writ on history's page,
More hurts than could, a second chance, assuage –
So passed your time, in anguish mixed with joy;
Self-laughter, as the means to now employ:
To see your life, (all lives), some cosmic joke,
Endured by all who labour in its yoke –

And nearing end, the substance of those years,
Amount to what? Some hopes, some joys, some fears:
Some aspirations, never to be gained?
What cosmic joke, imperfectly explained?
What might we take, when all is swept away
And clouds roll back, to show us our last day?
The stage is hushed, there will be no encore –
So came your time, in time, then nothing more.

* * *

As Grief's to part, so Grief's the heart, we bared
Upon your leaving, for the times unshared:
Lost to the past, lost to the times to come,
Grief is the loss, to which the rest succumb.
It's for the void, the absence and the fear;
The taking for a reason, still unclear;
The why, and wherefore, of our little lives;
The where, and how, and what – we hope, survives.

Dedicated to my mother's courage and determination
in the playing out of her last years.

'Potted Plant': Pastel on cartridge paper, 1977

SUMMER HAIKU, MT NEBO

Still, hot, dawn haze sings
chirping Mexican hat-wave –
Cicada chorus.

MAPLETON DAWN

Silence is roaring
on my still hill this morning –
A hot day coming?

'Butterfly Bower': Rollerball, wash & whiteout pen on Arches paper, 2006

FINGAL FEBRUARY 2004

Sullen scrub stillness –
Shimmering blue bowers bring
butterfly blessings.

AUTUMN TANKA

Approaching autumn,
leaves and blossoms still arrive
on trees near my home –
Fruit ripening, leaves falling
and still, fresh new growth arrives.

A SONG OF YEARNING

In the belly of the world
there sleeps a dream, they but forgot.
The world remembers, knows and dreams –
a dream-song spun, from star to stream;
in shifting grass, the stillness of
a perfect dusk and dawn-washed clouds –
the very breath of being.

Being – of a shifting dream,
that all remember, save those in reason bred –
in resonance of reason, one waking dream forgot.
And darkness builds –
ten thousand, thousand frames of light
in cities darkness, glowing bright:
containments of each lost soul's dream
that stillness in night's depth redeems.

In solitude, they hear it yet:
the unsaid yearning, sense of loss –
that something, all have but forgot.
Behind each window, glowing bright:
lone shadows move, linked by the night
and stirrings of vague memory
of what ... they know not what it meant,
before the fall, from consciousness
and grace.

CONTRAST THIS WAVE

Contrast this wave of subsea spawning,
rushing to a shore still dawning –
Surging promises of doom,
visited on third-world shores:
left its mark for evermore.

Homes and holdings, scant but precious,
swept aside in tidal rush –
and as the kraken retrogresses,
remnants wallow in the slush.
But Oh! But Oh! The human cost –
The lives in one wet moment lost!
The final score defies the count
as hundreds, in their thousands, mount.
The world-heard cries of inundations,
thrown out from earth's poorest nations,
shocks the ear, the heart, the mind –
And still, the final death-toll climbs.

Contrast this wave, the aftermath:
nations of the world take heart,
rush assistance, gifts of aid,
to lands laid bare, by sea-born swathe –
Save pestilence, wet-filth and thirst,
the horrors of the dead:
the first to feel the rigours.
Calm descends – A people stunned,
count their dead, collect possessions:
so little left from little –
And simple lives, so simply lost:
lost forever in the wash
of one, great sweeping ripple.

Contrast this wave, this subsea spawn –
Contrast this storm, whose wave was born
to contrast brave humanity,
whose home became an inland sea,
locked by levees, might and substance –
Still, none might redeem them.

This, no surging behemoth,
but harpies, venting all their wrath:
this storm swept all before her –
A yielding ocean gaining strength,
suppliant, followed down the length
of that great southern seaboard.
Prepared they were, precautions taken;
yet helpless still, stood by the nation,
watching devastation taking hold –
Whilst hundreds, in their thousands fled,
still many, in their thousands dead,
were taken to the fold.

Contrast this wave, the days that follow –
The great man in sweet torpor wallows,
waiting for his moment.
In arrogance, he waits their plea:
whose home became an inland sea –
And Oh! And Oh! The country's cost:
the property and oil drums lost!
Looting, plunder, rape and death
bestowed on those the waters left –
Land of Plenty! Home of The Free!
Is this then, Prosper's Legacy –
To foster Greed and Anarchy?

'Athenium Wind Harp': Screenprint on Arches Dessin paper, 1983

IN THE AFTERMATH

In the aftermath of plenty,
all the citadels of plenty fall
in clouds of death, from which none crawl –
Save those to wail, and beat the breast, to cry
that justice must be done, and justly so:
for innocents, (not innocence),
were lost today –
And innocents shall lose tomorrow.

In the aftermath of reason,
all the gods of reason gone –
A brooding world, in madness waiting,
breeding such an undertaking:
the paper house of cards imploded,
as petals of decay unfolded,
stamens of their host left crying:
heartbeat of a culture dying –
Pandemic feasting on its host,
as congress prayed to Holy Ghost –

And ganglions have taken hold,
in prophesies so long foretold:
that thus, would end an era.

      * * *

In the aftermath of horror,
all barriers to horror fall,
as packages of death arrive
in dust, designed to over-ride
complacency and safety –
The die-hard message rolls with ease:
the media inured, to please
an audience of cult.

In the aftermath of avarice,
its culture, long-distended
to bursting-point, the strong anoint
the 'have', and 'have-nots' singled out,
with lines of want, and wanting-not,
defying comprehension –
It's no small wonder, that this plunder
drives our earth with all its worth
to melt-down paranoia.

      * * *

In the aftermath of carnage,
all vetoes placed on carnage fail –
So might and freedom may prevail,
protect the world from further actions
practiced by ungodly factions:
pimpernels in purdah.
The coalition's hounds unleashed,
while stakes of play are now increased:
with theories of intrigue abounding,
preys they seek, elude their hounding.
Resources tried, in vain they seek
to trap him, like a lover, who
when passion as it does, grows weak,
shape-changes to another.

In the aftermath of passion,
all the flush of passion fades –
A brave new venue fills blue screens
with vision of night raids –
A brave new villain takes the stage,
the focus of this footage:
game-boy war-games, nightly played –
No weapons found, the fiend's displayed,
dragged out from ravaged wreckage.
And vindicated now, they claim,
(mythologies glossed over),
reluctant order is maintained:
an interim, so highly strained,
as victors take possession.

In the aftermath of victory,
all sweet smell of victory flies –
A new world order, friable,
fends off hints of lies:
in righteousness, the gods take seat
to meet once more, at summit's peak;
assess the threat of terror –
And terror strikes once more, again;
its echoes tremor through the glen –
Such was expected: just not, when.
Thus galvanized, cold blood in thighs,
strict measures must be rendered:
quell all freedoms, which may give rise
to incidents so dreaded.

* * *

In the aftermath of terror,
all footholds found in freedom, slide –
Most citizens have naught to fear,
if citizens have naught to hide –
Save those who fail and pay the cost,
of freedom, (for protection), lost:
To languish in Orwellian dreams –
This world, no longer what, once seemed.

'Dorothy Thorogood WWII':
Aquarelle graphite pencil & wash on cartridge paper 2014

A PLAY ON PLAY

Oh, we are both quite mad, we said –
The thoughts that whisper through our head;
The urge to make of words, some play
Of fancy, fact, or simply fun:
To ponder on the perfect pun –

To rut about in rhyme and reason,
Shooting rhythm out of season;
Stalking down the mind-shy stanzas,
Seeking questions in the answers:
Hunting our elusive prey –

But where's the profit line, you say?

ON RAINY AFTERNOONS

Some rainy, fog-swathed afternoons
when all is bound in silence,
save muffled patters, as the leaves
sound through thickened air

with branches sighing,
stirred by breezes hardly-there;
save these, the only sound:
one's heartbeat, keeping time –

And time stands still, embraces all
the time one ever had ... and more.

GEISHA TANKA

By darkness profiled:
beauty in the cinema
and soft scent lingers.
She weeps and touches her eye –
Sweet ukiyo-e moment.

'Maurine': Coloured pencil on coloured Ingres paper, 1974

IT CAME UPON A MIDNIGHT CLEAR

It came upon a midnight clear,
in hidden hymning; psalms and silent litany,
arising from the hearts of men,
unbidden and unvoiced – lest doubt and fear
should seize their hearts, should hold dominion:
make of their might a mockery –

The very gifts that set them free
to squander Man's impunity:
fragile rights, that they in freedom
took for granted, held so dear,
that none but gods, should beg their pardon –
of no thing else, have cause for fear.

It came upon a midnight clear –
from dawn 'til midnight, media's means,
flood the senses, fill mute heads,
with doom-fraught litanies of fear:
pandemics, bombings, siren screams
exhort the world to fear and dread.

* * *

Awakened by the fear, Man's bred,
an Earth alive, (Man treats as dead) –
alive with power to end his scheming;
end the misuse, lack of care –
and caring not for sirens screaming,
stirs, her warning to declare:

'If fear and terror form Man's focus,
so, they should, embrace his locus –
From the barrel, springs the fuse
that Man might use, and so, abuse
this Earth that holds him dearly –
To the well-spring, hangs the rope
that Man might use, to draw up hope;
to mend his Earth sincerely.'

* * *

It came upon a midnight clear –
These times, when fear all else outsells,
makes it a tool, laconic:
from pills and potions, household spells;
to losing freedoms, rights held dear,
through forging rules, draconic.

Fear is an instinct, in its place,
essential to the human race
(and every other creature);
but common use to sell coercion,
every day, in every version,
haunts Man's very culture:

It's gross misuse from pole to soul,
creates a world, no longer whole –
In the portal, sits the key
all men may use, to set all free;
to mend this world completely –
In the Earth, resides the power,
to drive the miscreant from his tower;
re-form the world discreetly.

* * *

It came upon a midnight clear,
that Man could sing a song of grace;
own his fear, and wear it, with his clothing –
give it back its rightful place;
its image, on cave walls adhere,
accepted, free of loathing.

If fear's misuse could be reduced,
Man's mother Earth, might be induced
to still her restless stirring –
Reality's what Man creates,
wherein his focus most relates,
with images recurring.

* * *

So, sing, upon a midnight clear,
a theme, the image to maintain,
of faith, in joy and beauty –
Faith in the well-spring, to sustain –
Belief, in the emboldened duty,
to cherish Earth and hold her dearly,
proclaiming to the midnight clearly:
there's naught to fear on Earth, but fear.

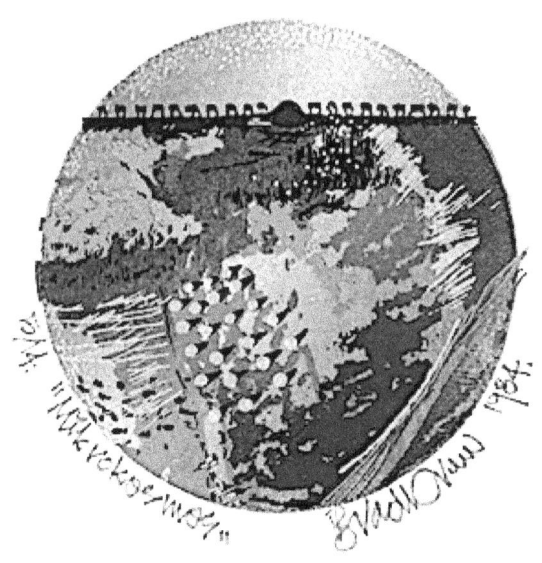

'Microcosmos': Screenprint on Arches Dessin paper, 1984

'Teddy Tanner': *Graphite block on cartridge paper, 2013*

TIME SLIPS THE WARP

Time slips the warp, where time and timely place
co-mingle on the loom of space laid bare
and each thread slips the cloth where shadows fade
(the world seen edgewise in a strand of hair).
On my event horizon's interface
what now seems convex was before, concave -
and all good reason and good sense efface.

Twice paradoxed within a field of grace,
twin singularities urge dreams to dare
and each dream slips the cloth that time upbraids
(the world lost edgewise in a dark-sunned pair).
On my event horizon's interface
all shadows cast and passed in space-time fade -
and all good reason and good sense efface.

Time slips the warp wherein your voice relates,
co-mingling on the loom that fate lays bare
and each word slips the cloth where dreams reside
(illusion lodging in a place none dare).
On my event horizon's interface
all boundaries of space and time subside -
each moment merging at one point of grace.

Twinned irises with depth where time abates
turn in a dance no quantum could prepare
and each step strips the cloth, its fabric frayed
(the fool's an angel lacking cause to care).
On my event horizon's interface
assumptions of what's probable abrade -
and all good reason and good sense efface.

Time slips the warp where time and seemly grace
entangle on the loom of space laid bare
and each move shifts the cloth the wise evade
(the fool lifts shadows where none others dare).
On my event horizon's interface
the vortex dancing with your eyes persuades
to all good reason and good sense efface.

MUTE CELLS CRY OUT

Mute cells cry out to catch again the dew,
call out the dawn to free the fleeting night
as mute, they throng among the blessed few.

In silence, led by thirsts as they accrue
in waiting on this first spring blush of light,
mute cells cry out to catch again the dew.

Dawn garners hope to feed the pulse, pursue
the promised hint of winter in its flight
as mute, they throng among the blessed few;

lean hillsides rush to herald by their hue,
spring's flush, as growing in their purpose might
mute cells cry out to catch again the dew

and parched thirsts drink, neglected cells imbue
the residues of winter in its flight,
as mute, they throng among the blessed few.

Should seasons fail, their bright gifts then eschew:
still calling for a cause to give delight,
mute cells cry out to catch again the dew

and urge the hillsides, not to once subdue
relief they found an instant in their sight,
as mute, they throng among the blessed few.

While patiently, they wait again their cue
to welcome in a spring ablaze with might,
mute cells cry out to catch again the dew
as mute, they throng among the blessed few.

[An extended villanelle]

WHAT CAUSED THE STATESMEN ALL

What caused the statesmen all, to go away;
   to leave affairs of state to rogues and fools
   who build a future tainted by dismay,
   foresight and wisdom absent from their tools?
What left us with so very little choice;
   who at the ballots, is there to give hope
   and through the shadows, guide us by their voice,
   convince us of ability to cope?

Well-meaning men, believing they could fly
   and finish hard, the race they chose to run,
   too late have found they ventured far too high,
   their feathers softened, broken by the sun.
Where are the men of substance at the helm
   whom greed or vanity shan't overwhelm?

[A Shakespearean sonnet]

'Teddy & Rose': Pencil on cartridge paper, 1976

RETRIEVAL FRAGMENT

To sleep within a bog, beneath a cairn:
the gift of being human, simply man.
But internment in a hollow log:
to rest as some bright totem
and have such friends as they would place
your remnants, borne aloft in grace,
as one who shared not in their blood
but shared their brotherhood and love –

To such degree accord respect,
that your remains, they could bedeck
and bear in sorrow deeply-felt,
within a tree trunk held aloft –
embalmed within, described without,
in symbolism scribed with pride:
in language of an ancient race,
forever more your soul embrace.

To be so loved, to be a part
of people's dreaming, sacred heart –
this world could hold like reverence
for superficial difference
where sameness lives beneath the skin
and blood flows from a common spring.

Some thoughts, following a sensitive documentary on the burial of a white helicopter pilot, dear, through his friendship and service, to an aboriginal community in The Gulf country.

REVISITING'S A TURNING IN THE MIND

Revisiting's a turning in the mind
   to regions where mind ought not wish to go;
   to pace again those paths akin in kind
   to patterns we should, in good sense, now know.
Returning to the space which we once left;
   repeating of the patterns we once knew
   is not designed to heal a soul bereft
   nor lead us from the place we should eschew.

Re-written scripts replace the tapes we score;
   the moment moves on at an unseen pace,
   brings comprehension we cannot ignore
   in seeking out our own small point of grace.
Revisited's another time's tabloid:
   read it with care, or otherwise avoid.

[A Shakespearean sonnet]

'St Mark's Square Venice': Rapidograph on tracing paper, 1983

DUSK HAIKU

My dog fleas herself
In time to frog serenades –
Dusk on a spring day.

'My Sister Bronwyn': Pencil on cartridge paper, 1977

FOR MAURIE –
15 OCTOBER 2006

A gentle soul once gently filled this space,
Was known by all to some or more degree –
Too late perhaps, we recognize his grace.

Bookshelf to bar and back, each day his pace
Belied the truth that few might truly see –
A gentle soul once gently filled this space.

Too often, kindness has an unseen face,
Consideration looks for no decree –
Too late perhaps, we recognize his grace.

Though scorned or loved, some truths cannot efface
The truth that lived and loved for all to see –
A gentle soul once gently filled this space.

So now he's gone and empty seems this place
He occupied so quietly and free –
Too late perhaps, we recognize his grace.

It's often when one's gone without a trace,
We yearn to know the depths we did not see –
A gentle soul once gently filled this space;
Too late perhaps, we recognize his grace.

[A villanelle]

'Maurie': Conte crayon on Fabriano paper, 2015

HOW DEFTLY RUN

How deftly run
the ruminations of a twilight –
Locked, as twilights do,
between the margins of two worlds.

Greens flush the day's last rush
as hollows deepen, shadows lengthen –
Soft ambers overwhelm these hills
as glowing fades to autumn twilight

And greys of evening slip the day
to cloak the path to midnight –
All colours soften on the road
through sundown, and beyond.

'Clouds at Dusk': Pen & wash on Arches paper, 2006

HAIKU ON RISING

Sunbeam through cloudbanks –
Which is it to be today,
My autumn hilltop?

THE DAY AFTER HAIKU

Steady grey daybreak –
Distant spatters on rooftops
Talk of her absence.

HOW CAME WE TO THIS DARKNESS?

How came we to the darkness of this place again?
How leisurely the seams do fall apart
and frayed threads lose their grip on all that's bright ...
For bright you were – twice-met it seems – or more?

How swiftly-spent, the margins of the self do blur –
do shift the threads that bind them, shift and fade.
The carousel will turn, another blur descend the stair ...
A frozen moment, played out for all time.

And so to grief, again we turn,
in sorrow's loss, the past to burn –
but what should past become once more, the now –
encounter dragons we had thought long-slain,
to find the dream, long-lost and spent ...
The present, one more stain?

How came we to the stillness of this place once more?
This instant's keening lost again to time –
one moment's keening song, the past to chide ...
All efforts at a present, fresh, deride.

And swiftly-gone, the heartbreaks and the loves long-spent –
infinity's swift instant evermore ...
For some, life is a moment from a past replayed –
the carnival's mad frenzy writes the score.

'Jim': Conte crayon on cartridge paper, 2008

A FENG SHUI CLEARING

Last season's lillypilly
had overhung and overgrown
my relationships corner –
and leaf mulch covered its heart ...
fat, dark worms had prospered
whilst one white, lazy centipede,
assuming kingship of the dank and dark,
presided in sloth-like majesty ...
and over all hung, the heavy stench
of feline dung, deposited
by next-door's newfound cat.

Yesterday,
in early-winter optimism ...
strange time of year for this,
I must admit ... but then,
admissions have become an easy thing ...
and if not now, then when?
Yesterday, I pruned and raked –
opened up a corner in my heart,
let in the light of optimism and intent –
cleared the ground and aired the earth.

And today ...
symbolically, I've cleared the path
and freed the gate, built upon
its two-fold purpose ...
invited in fresh love.
Tomorrow, I'll add lights
set to show the way at night –
for whom? I've no idea –
perhaps it's just for me.

TWIN EAGLES RISE

Twin eagles rise through half-light skies,
chase late November's sullen afternoon
to drop, bank, soar – to sweep and rise again –
grace dusk-stained embers of this fading day
with winds just right, to bear the might
of wedge-tailed majesty ... and death.

Death on a rising updraft glides
and soars above the last-light valley:
last for one, whose end has come –
mute benediction, signed in stealth
and shifting shadows, in the blush –
last flush, of gold and crimson on the hills.

Death down the spiraling updraft slides,
drawn through the five-hued talons of his eyes
to prey who waits him, calls him down,
tolled by the knell the cattle wear ...
at forest edge, on hillock's last illumined rise,
sudden and unseen, drops death.

The hill falls still, as homeward cattle bound,
peal out the ending of another day, and life:
a lowing hymn marks out their hoofsteps,
deep and mild. Light fades –
the updrafts falter and are gone –
gone too, the pinioned majesties of air.

'Over Sir John's Wood': Pencil study for screen print, 1980

SONG FOR A FLAT WORLD

They told me that the world be flat,
that there be dragons
and after them, be monsters.
Venture past a certain point ...
all else will fall away.

Yet, like reborn Columbus,
I've set my sails and headed east:
one compass bearing all I need ...
some landfall ... and the promise
of the sought-for new world, calls.

Fair such skies as beckon, lead
into the grail-lit morning;
and fair the song the trade winds sing
so softly through our rigging;
and fair the course that's set;

and fair the seas to follow ...
some landfall on a promised shore
beyond the flat edge world.
Dare to venture past this point:
all else will fall away.

'Ship in Storm': Rollerball & whiteout on rusted Arches paper, 2006

ANOTHER SONG OF SONGS :
'Oh my Beloved, my Song of Songs, and you, the Songstress ...'

CANTO I

Hearken, oh my Love, for I bear no falseness in my words,
   nor with flattery beguile;
   and I know, am well-aware in truth, the timing of our years.
Nor do I speak from kindness, nor in mute consideration –
   this is my Song of Songs
   and is in truth, my sole account of thee ...
Not through rose glasses I, but rather, what my heart knows
   of thee; and what I see, hear, taste, touch, and smell –
   for I am well-pleased, and humbled, and beset by thee.

My Love, you are comely, fair and full with love and joy;
   you are wisdom and mystery to me –
   good sense and soft enigma.
Tender, and terrible of influence, you pervade
   and navigate my sleep;
   drain me of sound reason –
I am lost and helpless before thee
   and I know no more ... no, naught ...
   of life before you entered.

My Love, you are my skin, my joy, my fear
   and daily, the thought of you
   haunts my every moment.
You are my life, my inner substance,
   my suspended sentence
   and my welcome cause.
I could not, would not,
   cage your freedom song
   nor rob thee of its content.

And oh, my Love, my heart delights most
   in your glance
   and your smile lights up my being.
You are my raison d'etre; and my heart would ever chase you,
   sans raison ...
   for you are my night and day, my moon and sun,
My every breath of being ... I am eclipsed,
   and I discover
   I am incomplete without thee.

My Love, my Heart, you inhabit my dreams and strew my paths
   with the leaves and litter of longing, while my heart groans
   and breaks, before and upon each parting ...
Thus likewise, sighs and leaps my heart upon each meeting
   and I am ever well-favoured;
   and so amply-blessed.
You mark the measures of my sleep and dreams
   and magnify my green and clumsy foolishness;
   in foolishness, I say too much ... too much I fear, of me ...
   and ask too much of thee.

'Lions of St Mark's Venice': Pencil & ink on tracing film, 1983

CANTO II

It is autumn, oh my Love. Our years are numbered:
   the month is April...
   and July is distant still.
Autumnal bloom enfolds you (as, wish I might, would I),
   and you are sweet,
   and filled with sugars of the season.
Your skin is soft and velvet with all fullness
   of the season's bloom, fragrant and enticing;
   and I cherish the linger of its smell, held
   in linen of the bed and bath, you leave behind thee.

Your breath is sweet, your kiss elusive; I pursue them
   both, with ardency and sweet desire... I chase them
   like some shy doe, for a single moment's touch.
Your touch, thrills me and delights;
   gentle and tender,
   your fingers are soft and loving.
You are all gentle shyness of the forest doe, my Love:
   and I would not chase thee down nor cage thee...
   rather, tend your needs, nourish and protect thee.

Look upon me, oh my Love and smile, that I might see
   the loving favour in thine eyes; for thine eyes
   are two soft pools over the gentle fervour of thy heart.
Look upon me, oh my Love and smile, that I might taste
   the fullness of thy lips; for thy lips are soft,
   generous, and breathe the air of love.
Your breath and love are soft and sweet;
   precious as rare oils and spices... breathe into me
   your essence, and the incense of thy love.

Show only to me, your morning, and your evening face
   in all its purity and freshness...
   for it is the face I most treasure and adore.
Show only to me, your private face, the first and last
   of each day's wearing... for it is your most lovely,
   fresh and youthful face,
   and wears the cleanness of your love.
I see your morning, evening, private face, oh my Love,
   with all the jealousy of a lover...
   mine alone to cherish, and I would not share its beauty.

Hold me and enfold me, oh my Love,
   store me in your secret places
   and lay me up for winter, should it ever come...
And I will be warm coals to ease your chill;
   my arm, a safe place and a pillow, for your head;
   my body's curve, thy shelter from the wind.
It is autumn, my Love... thy season's bloom is greater
   than the months and years that fed it; I would store it
   in the safe place of my heart,
   when winter winds might blow.

'My Great Aunt, Effie Higgenson':
Conte crayon on cartridge paper, 2013

CANTO III

I watched for my Beloved, twenty-thousand nights;
    waited on her, called upon her name,
    which none did know...
And searched I every lane, outpost
    and byway for her sign.

And lo, I followed and pursued her shadow
    down the byways and backwaters of my life,
    to no avail and no effect.
So many times mistook another for her,
    started at a promise, unfulfilled and incomplete.

I asked in turn, Are you she, for whom
    my soul does hunger, and does yearn...
    are you my heart's great longing and desire?
And she said, Maybe... or, No, but I will stay awhile
    to comfort thee... but nothing more.

I thought I saw her once and chased her shadow;
    chased and lost, then chased again...
    each time, the shadow lengthened,
And my heart lost heart and closed upon itself,
    for still the name, which none did know.

Where are you, my Loved and Longed-for One,
    in whom I do believe and trust,
    and where do you reside,
    these twenty-thousand nights
I've waited for you, called your name,
    the name which none do know?

CANTO IV

Hearken, oh my Love, for you are comely
   and more than passing-fair to me; though I know
   full-well, the truth in timing of our years.
Oh, you are spring in autumn,
   and I would follow thee with faith,
   beyond the end of days.
Your eyes are two soft and gentle pools
   where drowns my heart; with cheeks and lips,
   lush with the bounty of the season's ripeness.

I would taste the fullness of your lips
   and draw into me,
   the sweetness of your breath;
For your lips are soft and your speech is sweet.
   Your voice is a balm unto my ears
   and your song, the transport of my heart.
I would hear thy voice
   and hold it to my soul,
   when all else fades, is gone.

Speak to me, my Love,
   that I might know your heart
   and hearken to its call.
Speak to me,
   that I might hear your voice
   and mark its music through my soul;
For thy speech is a sweet
   and gentle balm
   which holds me in its thrall.

Behold and listen ...
    the lark who thrills the glade,
    fills and binds the soul.
Sing with me, my Love,
    draw near to me
    and sing the balance of our days...
For you are a lark unto my life,
    evensong, and vespers
    for my timely day.

Hearken, oh my Love, for you are comely,
    and your voice,
    the joy of larksong fair to me;
Your eyes, two pools to plunge,
    and lips to breathe and taste,
    full transport for my soul;
Your breath as sweet as speech...
    the spikenard and balm
    to soothe my days.

CANTO V

I glimpsed her, then I found her,
    she whose name none ever knew.
And I drew her to me,
    that I might better see her face.
There, loveliness resides and has my heart,
    overtaken and undone.
And my heart leaps to her, sings in joy,
    then cries out in her absence.
Her name is Softness and Beauty,
    and I am forever lost.

CANTO VI

Beloved mine, you are all tenderness at once,
    and terrible... all terrible as an army
    that lays siege and sacks my nights;
For, sleep as I might, my heart does wake me
    to the drumroll of thy absence
    and my unslept longing knows no bounds.

Your image, person, and your voice,
    draw me from sleep and I am beset
    by the banners and the marching of your host.
You walk among my dreams, my Love,
    soft-shod and urgent
    and thy quiet footstep stirs my unquiet night.

Beloved mine, you tend the garden of my being;
    its beds are full to overflowing with the bounty
    of your fruit and blossoms.
You are the bee who tends, for you fertilize
    and feed my hunger; yet steal my appetite,
    shore up my zest for eating.

Come to me, my Love, and lie with me;
    lay off your siege and let your soft-shod footsteps
    pause and rest, spoon-wise, in mine.
Let the fullness of your autumn fruit,
    quench my thirsting mouth
    and quell my always hunger for thee.

Scatter your blossoms on my brow,
    oh sweetest Love, breathe your sleep
    and slumbering heart with mine...
In the rising and the falling of our breasts,
    decamp your army, cease your siege,
    and set the standard of your tenderness upon me.

CANTO VII

How beautiful you are, my Love;
    for you are more than passing fair
    and comely in your bearing.
Your very being, and your body,
    are a well-matched
    and fitting slipper unto mine...
We do wear each other, like fitting and
    well-tailored garments, cut and fashioned
    for all seasons and all weathers.
You are beauty, my Love,
    and you bring me to my knees,
    tear my heart asunder.

Your head is a chalice of goodness,
    crowned with wisdom.
Your head is a fine and delicate globe,
    wreathed by the wildness of your hair,
    a tangle of sacred and profane delights...
Your hair is a joy to me
    and your nose is fine and stately,
    in breath, so soft and sweet.
Your cheeks are high and rounded,
    set with smiling dimples,
    as ripe pomegranates.

Your eyes are deep with kindness
    and are two pools
    in which I sink to drown.
Your lips are generous
    and I would breathe the honey
    of your lips and tongue.
Your feet, are small and eloquent
    and I would kiss and swallow them,
    like words of love.
Your calves and thighs are slender saplings,
    and your buttocks,
    small and firm as apples.

Your navel is a jeweled thimble,
   set in the gentle swell;
   a small boat moored upon a gentle sea.
The gentle swelling of your belly
   is a soft basket;
   container of your warmth and goodness.
Your breasts are the bounty of two peaches,
   flowing and full
   with autumn juices...
And you are full with love for me,
   and my pulse quickens
   with your warmth.

Oh, my Love of Loves, you fill me with desire,
   hasten my breath,
   for my hand is want upon thee.
Your name is Softness and Beauty,
   Quickness and Desire...
   and I would fain lie with you,
   to be thy grist and core.
Would, that I could breathe your breath
   and share the beating of your heart.
   Lock me within thee, oh my Love,
   and never let me go;
For I am yours alone,
   I am your troth and would,
   that thou were truly pleased with me.

CANTO VIII

Hurry, oh my Love, and squeeze out
   the fullness of each moment
For I am your Love and have waited on you,
   called your name,
   these twenty-thousand nights...
And your name is Lovely, Beauty,
   Softness and Desire,
   and I am full, well-full, of thee.

Your name, which none could name,
   has marked me
   and is a seal upon my heart.
Your flame ignites my veins
   and will not let me rest,
   for you are lovely and do blind my sight.
All I am and would be,
   is in thee, my Love
   and you are my purpose and delight.

Come and twine with me, my Love;
   encompass me, hold me close,
   and spill the juices of our season...
For I will drink your heady wine,
   anoint you
   with the nectar of my being,
And I will cradle thee from the storm,
   my arm a pillow
   and a comfort to thy soul.

Speak to me, my Love, and call my name
   as I've called yours
   and shout, for all the world to hear.
Take my hand and clasp it to your heart,
   pull my arms about you;
   swallow my mouth and drown me in your fire,
For I am mad-crazy for you,
   and would have thee melt for me.

Clasp my hand and walk with me, my Love,
    and wear each moment in your breast...
For I would fain share,
    and hold each moment with you,
    adore you to the end.
You are contentment and great joy to me,
    oh my Love... my reason
    and the absence of all reason.

*With respectful apologies
to Solomon, King.*

'Lions of St Mark's': Pencil & ink on tracing film, 1983

'Standing Woman': Sharpened stick, ink & charcoal on cartridge paper 2009

YOU ARE MY SONG

You are my evening and my autumn song
   and you would be the last I'd wish to sing;
   as autumn moves to winter, short or long –
   I'll sing you still, whatever time may bring.
I'll sing your song with passion and with joy,
   with tenderness and sweet gentility –
   and if time's passage should the voice destroy,
   your melody will linger, clear and free.

Should you consent to hold me and my love
   against your heart and ear for all of time,
   your song, your name, will charge my heart above
   all others, and to yours, my voice will climb.
For you remain my substance, my delight:
   you are the song that fills me, day and night.

[A Shakespearean sonnet]

'Seated Woman': Sharpened stick, ink & charcoal on cartridge paper, 2009

I THINK YOU HAVE, MY HEAD UNDONE

I think you have, my head undone:
by all that's light and all that's bright,
I know, my heart, you've overrun –

for as your landfall hove in sight
you furled my sails, some twelve months past
with all your light, by all that's bright.

Though fly our days and seasons fast,
moored in these new world's waters sound,
you've furled my sails, these twelve months past.

Much goodness in your soul rebounds
and in your presence, I am blessed –
moored in these waters, safe and sound.

I know you have, my heart possessed:
yours is the grail that brings me light
and by your presence, I am blessed.

You show me beauty, as my right –
I feel you have, my past undone:
yours is the grail that lights my night.
I know, my heart, you've overrun.

[A terzanelle: derived from the villanelle and terza rima forms]

'Head of a Man': Sharpened stick & ink on cartridge paper, 2009

UPON THE NEW WORLD LANDFALL

A safe and pleasant mooring, sheltered and abundant –
Furled the sails and anchored deep,
The sirens' song lost to their sleep
Our ship rides gently on the swell of harboured rest
And all around, our new world's charms attest
The rightness of our landfall –

At harbour's edge, so spreads our landfall verdant
This promised shore, this haven, keep –
Both Eden, and a place to reap
The harvest of a journey started long years past
When different helmsmen stood before the mast
To hold us each in thrall.

For you alone, are journey's end –
Your verdant country, I will tend
With love and dedication –
Our damaged paths and fields to mend,
Along your ways I'll gladly wend
With easy step, forsaking hesitation.

'St Mark's Square' Detail: Rapidograph on tracing paper, 1983

A POEM FOR VALENTINE

The season's February and Cupid's come
in winged haste, all quiver and bow –
Summer wanes through her last glow.

Hart, hare and hound retreat, as kite
soars high to cry the season's exit
to Autumn and the Fall –

As once did Psyche's sisters fall –
Eros-lured, in other times
and half a world full distant.

In our Autumn, Spring revives again,
entreats both wary and the not-so –
to once again be mine and share
the sweetness of this arrow drawn.

'Potted Plant': Rapidograph on cartridge paper, 1977

THREE YEARS OUT

Three years from landfall on that promised shore
when hearts were light and buoyant to the cause
and verdant through the mists, new Eden rose
around us, fresh with lushness and so clean
the air itself, glowed with an inner light –
so came safe harbour, comfort, pure and bright.

No place is free of goblins, nor of ghosts –
the same proved true for this new world, our host:
for as we staked our claim and marked our plots
faint ghosts were glimpsed to dart at vision's edge;
and as we plumbed and charted out our shore
discovered shoals and reefs, but little more.

We chart our waters carefully, now we know
and watch for where waves break amid safe flows;
look out for goblins in the fairy dells
or ghosts, whose whispers break the season's spell;
for true our landfall is, and fair our barque –
this journey's ours – how could we disembark?

'Lighthouse, Byron Bay': Notebook pencil sketch, 1979

'My Great Uncle, Robert Higgenson in Flanders':
Graphite stick on cartridge paper, 2013

A POEM FOR CHRISTMAS

Morning – and insistent dawn
slips past shutters, dreams and sleep.
I sense your stirring, tuned to mine –
your gentle breathing – and I wonder
whether this waking heat is yours
or that of oncoming day?

Yet another solstice done,
days shorten on the path to autumn
and beyond – it's almost Christmas –
while the gift you are, warms and heartens:
stirs daily, gratitude for your presence
through this Autumn of our seasons.

I watch your waking profile
and wonder at my own good fortune –
listen for the first birds' calling
late in this rising heat of day –
savour this season and our mountain,
to thank the world for who you are.

'Historishes Museum, Berne': Ballpoint pen on cartridge paper, 1976

AND OF CONTENTMENT ...

I witness summer winding down
as February sounds her last retreat
and this year's hares still find delight
in dandelions that grace our hill.

All summer, they have come to meet
and sample full, the weeds that crown
our slopes; dawn brings them there
and dusk returns them still.

No March hare madness this –
save quiet contentment in
familial ways and gentle bliss
as summer greets sweet autumn.

And of contentment, I am mindful
of her easy touch, as all my summers
roll off into one: sum and total
of those all, which came before.

So comes our southern Valentine
lazy with the last of summer's heat
to quietly have us all entreat –
as I do now – to ask you to be mine.

'Grail Image' Notebook study : Aquarelle stick graphite & wash, 2013

FOUR YEARS HAVE COME TO US

Four years have come to us and washed these shores
as varied as the tides, which in their surge
bear mostly treasured shells and little more –

We've seen our journeys into one, converge
despite some storm-front surges from the past
as varied as the tides, which by us, surge –

Our voyage, mainly smooth beneath this mast –
astern, the gentle passage of each now
in spite of storm-front surges from our pasts.

Since setting sail, four years have passed our bow
to run our length and sparkle in our wake
as churns astern, the passing of each now –

The purpose of this journey's no mistake
so we must trim our sails and fair seas urge
to run our length and sparkle in our wake –

For right, a voyage is, that would so merge
while years may come to us and wash our shores –
then as we trim our sails and fair seas urge
find mostly pretty shells and little more.

[A terzanelle: derived from the villanelle and terza rima forms]

'Head of a Woman' Detail : Rollerball & wash on Arches paper, 2009

ONE SEASON'S MOULD

Vinegar! ... And cloves! ...
For weeks, it's rained, or seems so
as the last of summer's breath lies heavy
burdens every mote that ever settled
on the contours of my home –
and spores spring forth in sudden places.

An host is come ...
entrenched its mould-spawned minions
encamped itself on bulwark and in hollow
laid siege, established beachheads
on my walls, my couch, my shoes, my belts!
The pungent, rotting–citrus bloom springs forth –
adorns them all.

In the village, townsfolk mutter
curse and throng the streets –
storm the shelves of pharmacy and hardware
both – for oil of cloves and vinegar
regroup for bleach in every form ...
as desiccator vendors rub their hands
and dehumidifiers thrum
to drain the hub of humid households.

These then, are the wages
of our mountaintop existence
lodged along the margins of the clouds –
responding to the fungal fugue
with seasonal insistence
we air our cupboards, stoke our fires
maintain the mushroom vigilance
our treasures to preserve.

'Mushrooms': Rollerball & wash on Arches paper, 2006

MUTE SUNFLOWERS FROM GREY ASHES

Mute sunflowers from grey ashes sadly rise
their benedictions, begging time to stall –
to see how reason from this world still flies

So brief, the time they had to realize
that time could end thus and bright darkness fall
whilst mute, would sunflowers from grey ashes rise

For in that instant, stripped of compromise
a final moment, from which none might crawl –
none witness for themselves, how reason flies

These scattered parts, confetti of their lives
adorn the landscape – silence to appall
as mutely, sunflowers from sad ashes rise

For while we argue where the true blame lies
news networks vie to hold us in their thrall –
convey how reason from this world now flies

Until another headline sounds its cries
and interests in the current banner pall
mute sunflowers will from ashes, sadly rise
to show how reason from this world still flies.

[A villanelle]

'Ravine': Pencil Notebook Study for Screenprint, 1979

'My Great Aunt, Mary Higgenson':
Conte crayon on cartridge paper, 2013

AS AUTUMN TURNS ...

As autumn turns to sleep with winter's years
   and friends recede as hailed by close of day
   we seek distractions to allay our fears
   that in the end we're little more than clay.
We look for what we might now leave behind
   convince ourselves that we might be revered –
   that much of it was not just in our mind
   but had a form more valued than was feared.

Spare us from dwelling in a pumped-up past
   reliving blown-out visions of our youth:
   false vanities devoid of power to last –
   mythologies which test the bounds of truth.
Wear old age with such modesty and grace
   vain foolishness in old age won't deface.

[A Shakespearean sonnet]

'Fruit Detail': Rollerball, felt pen, wash and ink on Arches paper, 2006

A SONNET FOR VALENTINE'S

This February has arrived, and still
   our own fleet hares return, to laze and graze
   the ever-constant haven of our hill.
Through mists and squall, they've come to grace this slope
   and brought the young, to share these joyous days
   which crown their own existence with such hope.

This week has seen them sportive, gay and light;
   to leap, spin, turn, cavort across the hill
   in mating-mad abandonment's fey flight
to garner all these joys at summer's end,
   ward off the threat of hoary winter's chill:
   such is the essence of the path I'd wend
to tarry with you for this little while
   and give you some cause, through the mists, to smile.

[A terza rima sonnet]

'St Mark's Square' Detail: Pen & ink on tracing paper, 1983

TO LATER FRIENDSHIPS

Friends come and go throughout the flux of life;
   they catch the sun, to shine and briefly flare
   but often, overtaken by some shade,
   they find themselves replaced by other cares:
these mostly not for reasons false or trite
   but simply time and distance, lets them fade.
   Nostalgia meanwhile, holds them in her arms,
   to hang them round our life, like chain-linked charms.

And then there are those others, coming late,
   as sparks to smoulder in the embers of our day:
   who through their strengths, will suffer no such fate;
   for you, my friend, will sidestep all the shade
wherein, for time and distance, others laid –
   thus, unforgotten, ever shall you stay.

'Seated Woman' Detail: Sharpened stick & ink on cartridge paper, 2008

'My Great Grandfather, Robert Higgenson Snr.':
Block graphite on cartridge paper, 2014

A POEM FOR JULY

At this time of year, I find I've now become
Aware of odysseys and voyages begun
And sailed, through latitudes and longitudes uncharted,
As questing eastwards, one reborn Columbus started –
Sailing far beyond the seas he knew,
Through seasons and through climes of changing hue.

When that new Columbus set out for the edge
Of reason, or the world he'd come to know;
Or when a latter-day Ulysses swore his pledge
To faithfully return at journey's close –
However might the surge of seas and currents flow,
This was the course, he so willingly, then chose.

Now, five years since our odyssey began
And three years since we furled our sails,
To cast our anchor, settle our new land;
Surmount with love, what storm-fronts may assail –
Thus, garner in the harvests of our joy,
Protect our haven and all means deploy,
To meld as one, the substance of our lives:
Plant out our plot, so naught but goodness, thrives.

'Lighthouse, Point Byron': Pencil notebook sketch, 1979

THREE NINDERRY TANKAS

Consigned for all time
Within these stocks, these mute rocks,
Rash Ninderry squats –
Contemplates eternity
And his ever-present past.

Sitting thus in stocks,
No birds sing to Ninderry,
Vilified and scorned –
He watches still, the lovers,
United by Maroochy's grief.

Still flows the river,
Sheds tears across the flood plain
From ranges to sea –
Scattered Coolum finds his rest;
Maroochy's grief, the waves attest.

'Mt Coolum & Beacons': Rollerball & whiteout on Arches paper, 2006

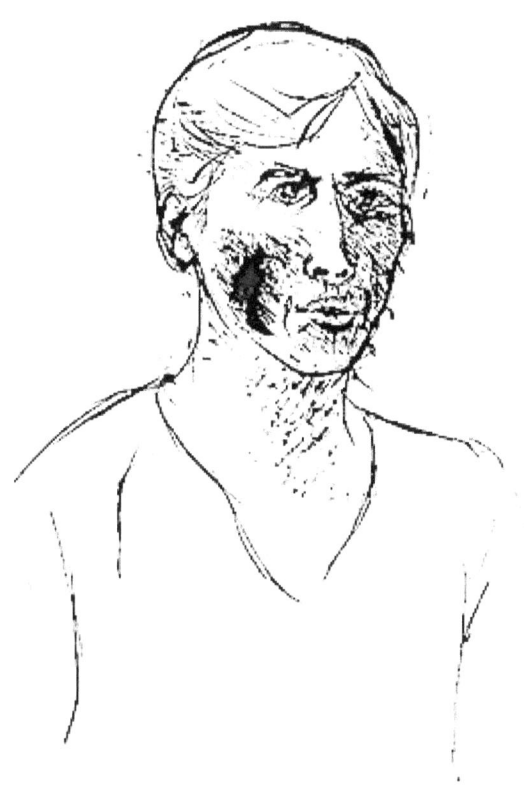

'Self Portrait 1983': Quill liner & Indian ink on Fabriano paper

Traces of a Life

www.ingramcontent.com/pod-product-compliance
Lightning Source LLC
Chambersburg PA
CBHW061948070426
42450CB00007BA/1095